GUITAR LEGENDS ALPHABET

Words by Robin Feiner

A is for Duane **Al**lman.
As leader of '60s rock giants,
The Allman Brothers Band,
'Skydog' uplifted his fans
with infectious licks and
dazzling slide guitar playing.
He was passionate, melodic
and so unique that he used
a glass bottle that once
contained cold medicine
as a slide!

Bb

B is for Jeff Beck.
'The Guv'nor' made his mark
playing in The Yardbirds, and
for Rod Stewart and Roger
Waters. Always surprising,
the British axeman would
frequently switch genres and
reinvent his sound at will.
In the '80s, he stopped using
a pick because he felt he
was wasting three fingers.

**C is for Carlos Santana.
This Mexican legend has an instantly recognizable guitar tone – fusing Latin and blues into one clean, smooth sound. Famous in the '70s with his band, Santana, and as a solo act in the late '90s, Carlos has won 10 Grammy Awards including Record and Album of the Year.**

D is for **D**avid Gilmour. 'Prog rock' would be nothing without Pink Floyd's David Jon Gilmour, who co-wrote classics such as 'Comfortably Numb' and 'Shine On You Crazy Diamond.' Known for his use of wailing delay and echo on Fender guitars, this legend was awarded an Order of the British Empire in 2003.

Ee

E is for **E**ric Clapton.
Known as 'God' to fans
and critics alike, this British
bluesman of Derek and the
Dominos and Cream is known
for his catchy melodies and
raw emotion. Clapton has
scored 17 U.S. Top 40 songs
in his career, including the
megahits 'Layla' and
'Tears in Heaven.'

Ff

F is for **F**rank Zappa. Quirky, avant-garde and as hilarious as he was brilliant, Zappa established himself as a truly unique artist over a 38-year career. His ability to write odd, jumpy solos, play unusual rhythms, and even compose entire symphonies saw him inducted into the Rock and Roll Hall of Fame in 1995.

G is for **G**eorge Harrison. The massive success of The Beatles is partly thanks to this British master's gorgeous melodies and legendary songwriting abilities. With George, every note counted, and his memorable, tasteful playing style crossed genres. Guitar lovers will never forget his masterpiece: 'While My Guitar Gently Weeps.'

H is for Jimi **H**endrix.
The undisputed best guitarist of all time, James 'Jimi' Hendrix demolished the foundations of rock 'n' roll with never before seen skill, and created never before heard sounds.
His performance at Woodstock is legendary, and setting fire to his guitar is one of music's most iconic moments.
An undeniable genius.

I is for Tony **I**ommi.
This lead guitarist of English superstars, Black Sabbath, joined vocalist Ozzy Osbourne to create a new genre of music. At the age of 17, 'Riff Lord' overcame losing the tips of two fingers to give the blues a dark, loud makeover, and suddenly, heavy metal was born. Legendary.

Jj

J is for Joni Mitchell.
Teaching herself to play, and
inventing her own harp-like
style, this iconic Canadian
singer—songwriter used her
guitar as a companion to her
soulful vocals. Her gentle
strength struck a chord with
women in the 1960s and 70s,
and she's paved the way for
female artists ever since.

K is for B.B. **K**ing. Dubbed 'The King of the Blues,' B.B. had a smooth interpretation of vibrato and string-bending skill. His ingenious use of silence between licks combined to create some of the most soulful blues guitar playing in history. Every young guitarist learns one or more of this legend's licks.

**L is for Les Paul.
So influential was this musical wizard that in 1952, he invented one of the most popular styles of guitar: the Gibson Les Paul. Thanks to this and other guitar-related inventions, Paul is the only person to enter both the Rock and Roll Hall of Fame and the National Inventors Hall of Fame.**

M is for **M**ark Knopfler.
As front-man for U.K. megastars,
Dire Straits, Mark Freuder
Knopfler finger-picked his way
to selling over 30 million copies
of the 1985 album, 'Brothers
in Arms.' Using his '61 Fender
Stratocaster, he wowed
audiences with a tasty blend
of rhythm and lead on classic
tracks like 1978's 'Sultans
of Swing.'

N is for Neil Young.
'The Godfather of Grunge'
is proof that you don't need
flash to be a guitar legend.
Nobody can express feeling
through playing like Young,
and his ability to create
simple, soul-crushing parts
on both acoustic and electric
guitar scored him 26 Grammy
nominations in 25 years.

O is for **O**rianthi.
Before this Australian phenom was 19, she'd already jammed with Steve Vai and Carlos Santana. After playing lead, crystal-studded guitar for Michael Jackson prior to his final epic concert, she became the go-to guitarist for artists including Alice Cooper and Carrie Underwood, and is one of the best players in the world.

Pp

P is for **Prince.**
A musical virtuoso whose magnificent guitar skills were only one aspect of his supreme overall talent, 'Prince' Rogers Nelson played funk rock with an otherworldly feel, emotion and personality. His flamboyant collection of guitars included purple-colored, leopard-printed and 'symbol'-shaped. This legend put the 'electric' in electric guitar.

Qq

Q is for **Q**ueen's Brian May. As lead guitarist and songwriter alongside Freddie Mercury, 'Bri' created entire guitar orchestras on one of the most popular songs of all time, 'Bohemian Rhapsody.' He built his legendary 'Red Special' electric with his father – a guitar designed to feed-back depending on air movement. Awesome!

R is for **R**obert Johnson. The man who started it all. Both blues and rock owe a great debt to this mysterious 1930s songwriter and his twangy acoustic playing style. His 29 recorded songs became legendary standards and influenced The Rolling Stones, Eric Clapton, Led Zeppelin and basically every guitarist since (whether or not they know it).

S is for Slash.
As lead guitarist for Grammy-nominated fivesome Guns N' Roses, Saul 'Slash' Hudson dominated '80s and '90s hard rock with his clean, mean solos and dirty, curly hair. Earning his nickname because he was always running (slashing) around, Hudson's work on 'November Rain' gave us the most memorable solo of the entire 1990s.

T is for Sister Rosetta Tharpe. 'The Godmother of Rock 'n' Roll' and her awe-inspiring guitar picking paved the way for Elvis Presley and Johnny Cash. As a person of color and the first gospel superstar, Tharpe broke down 1930s racial barriers by playing with white musicians, and pioneered the blues through her use of distorted electric guitar.

U is for **Uli** Jon Roth. This gifted guitarist rose to fame as part of Germany's number one rock band, The Scorpions, and soon became internationally recognized for his skillful improvising. He even invented the Sky Guitar, with a range that can go from violin to cello. Legendary!

V is for Eddie **V**an Halen. As frontman of '80s hard rock monsters, Van Halen, Eddie established himself as one of the fastest and most versatile guitar players ever. His jaw-dropping new uses for finger tapping and harmonics broke new ground and left listeners wondering how this legend does it!

W is for Nancy **W**ilson. Blending jazz and pop as lead guitarist for Heart, 'Fancy Miss Nancy' broke the mold in the '70s by grabbing the spotlight and topping the charts within a male-dominated genre. Her acoustic chops are some of the best ever, and her electric work on tracks such as 'Barracuda' are the very definition of legendary.

X is for Ale**x** Lifeson.
As guitarist for imaginative Canadian prog rock band, Rush, Lifeson mastered not only his electric and acoustic, but also played mandolin, bouzouki and sometimes two instruments at once! His ability to switch from slow and emotional to fast and ferocious continues to astound fans and critics alike.

Y is for Angus **Y**oung. Wearing his signature schoolboy outfit, Angus Young shook the world's largest stadiums with his awesome hard rock riffs and mesmerizing stage presence. As co-founder and lead guitarist for AC/DC, this legendary Australian rocker created the third highest-selling album and the seventh highest-selling tour of all time!

Zz

Z is for Led **Z**eppelin's Jimmy Page. If you don't know The Zep, you don't know rock. In 1968, Page formed music's most epic, immortal band and rocked the world with his legendary theatrics and eye-watering solos. Listen to 'Whole Lotta Love' and 'Stairway to Heaven' and bow down to the master. Rock on!

The ever-expanding legendary library

EXPLORE THESE LEGENDARY ALPHABETS & MORE AT WWW.ALPHABETLEGENDS.COM

GUITAR LEGENDS ALPHABET
www.alphabetlegends.com

Published by Alphabet Legends Pty Ltd in 2020
Created by Beck Feiner
Copyright © Alphabet Legends Pty Ltd 2020

978-0-6486724-7-0

ALPHABET LEGENDS